Hans-Günter Heumann

THE VERY BEST OF...
POP BALLADS

EASY ARRANGEMENTS FOR PIANO LEICHTE KLAVIERARRANGEMENTS

Bosworth Edition
part of The Music Sales Group

The Very Best Of Pop Ballads, H.-G. Heumann
Bosworth Edition

BOE7147
ISBN 3-937041-53-2
ISMN M-2016-5013-5

Inhalt/Contents

DREAMER
(OZZY OSBOURNE)

Words & Music by Marti Frederiksen,
John Osbourne & Mick Jones
Arr.: Hans-Günter Heumann

1. Gaz-ing through the win-dow at the world out-side,

won-der-ing will Moth-er Earth sur-vive,

hop-ing that man-kind will stop a-bus-ing her some-time.

drea - mer _____ I dream my life _____ a - way. _____

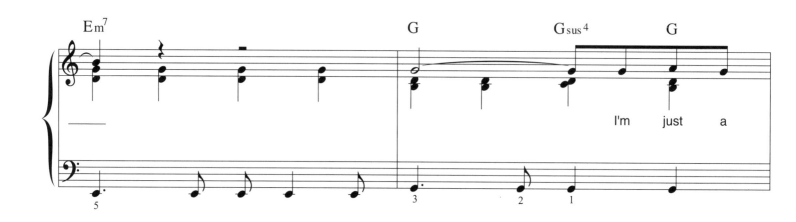

I'm just a

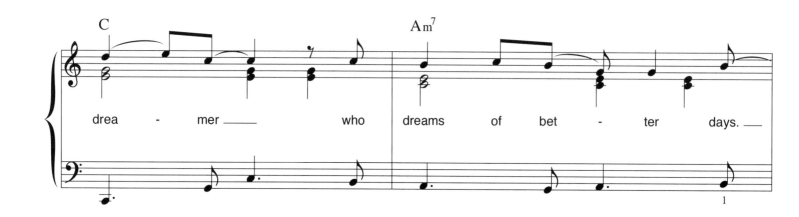

drea - mer _____ who dreams of bet - ter days. _____

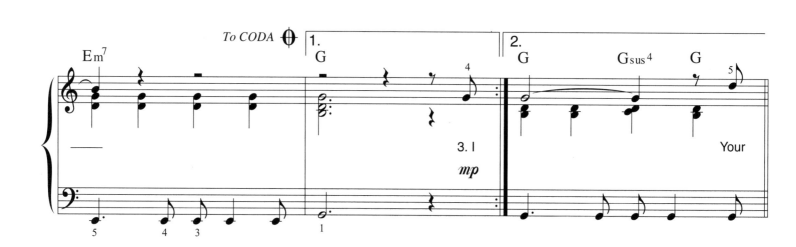

3. I

Your

I'm just a drea - mer who's

Verse 4:

If only we could all just find serenity,
it would be nice if we could live as one,
when will all this anger, hate and bigotry
be gone?
I'm just a dreamer, ...

BEAUTIFUL
(CHRISTINA AGUILERA)

Words & Music by Linda Perry
Arr.: Hans-Günter Heumann

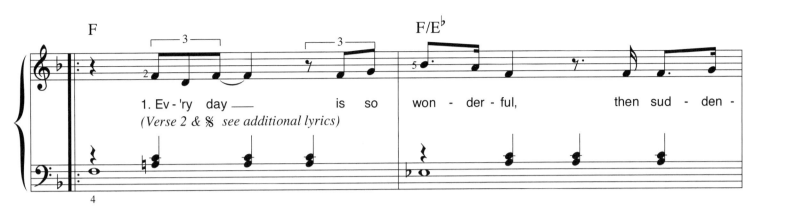

1. Ev - 'ry day ___ is so won - der - ful, then sud - den -
(Verse 2 & 𝄋 see additional lyrics)

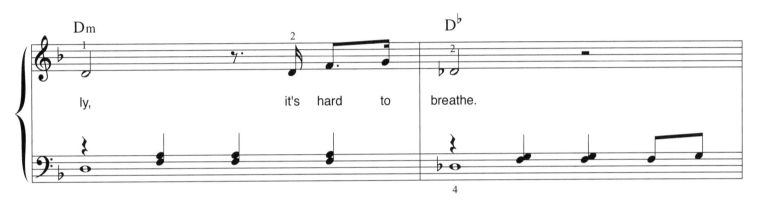

ly, it's hard to breathe.

Now and then, ___ I get in - se - cure from all the

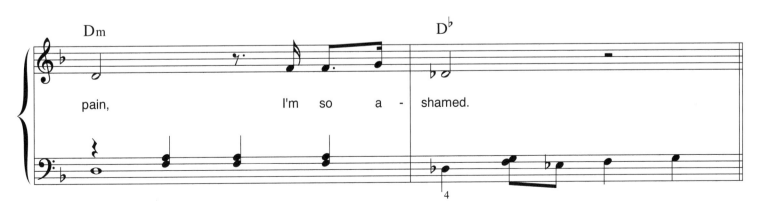

pain, I'm so a - shamed.

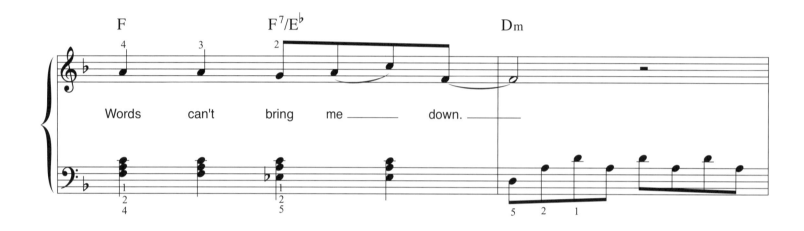

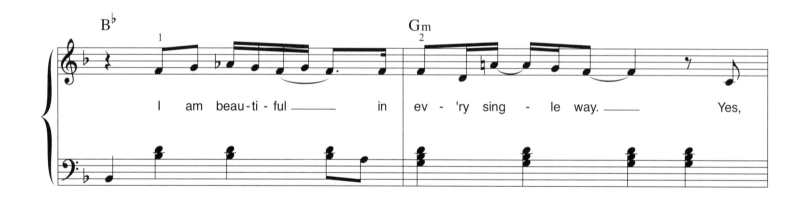

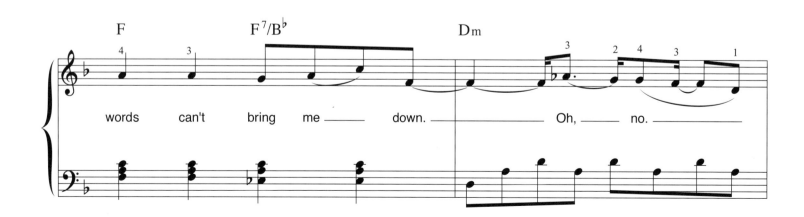

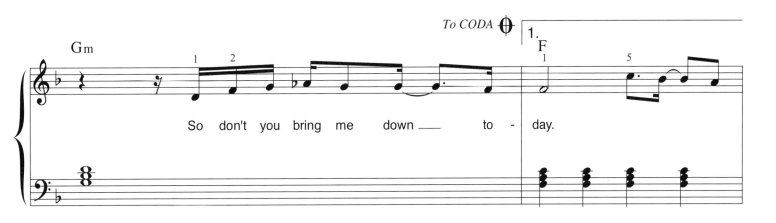

So don't you bring me down ____ to - day.

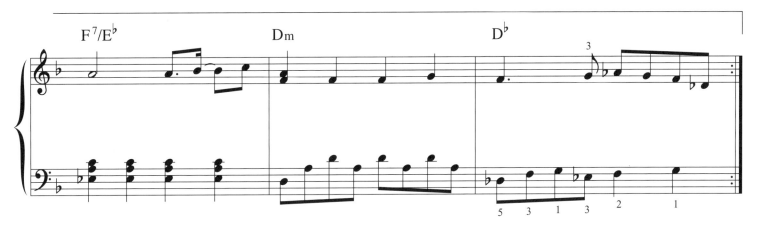

day. No mat - ter what ____ we do, _____ no mat - ter what ____ we say, ___

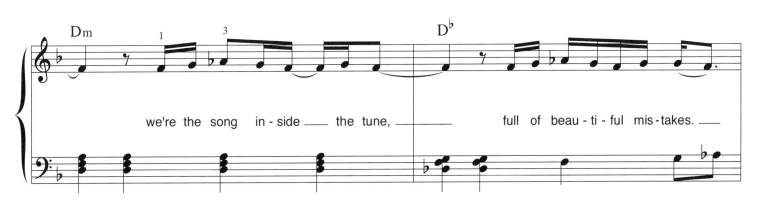

we're the song in - side ____ the tune, _____ full of beau - ti - ful mis - takes. ___

And ev - 'ry - where ___ we go, ___ the sun will al - ways shine, ___

___ but to - mor - row we might a - wake, ___ on ___ the oth - er side. ___

day.

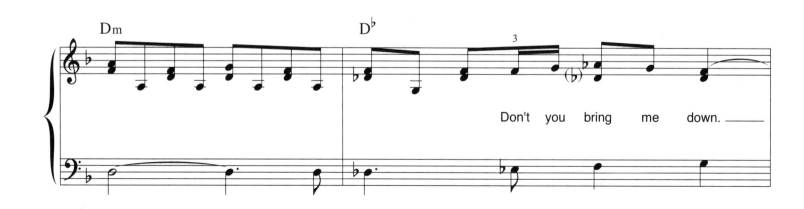

Don't you bring me down. ___

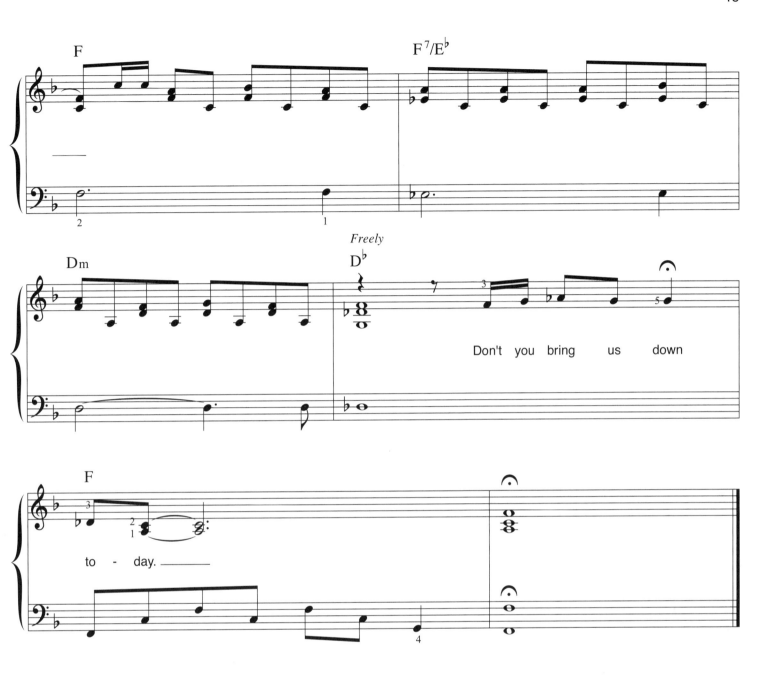

Verse 2:

To all your friends, you're delirious,
so consumed in all your doom.
Trying hard to fill the emptiness,
The pieces gone, let the puzzle undone,
that's the way it is?
'Cause you are beautiful, no matter what they say.
Words can't bring you down.
You're beautiful in ev'ry single way,
yes, words can't bring you down. Oh, no.
So don't you bring me down today.

No matter what we do, no matter what we say,
we're the song inside the tune, full of beautiful mistakes.
And ev'rywhere we go, the sun will always shine,
but tomorrow we might awake, on the other side.

𝄋

'Cause we are beautiful, no matter what they say.
Words won't bring us down.
We are beautiful, in ev'ry single way.
Yes, words can't bring us down. Oh, no.
So don't you bring me down today.
Don't you bring me down today.
Don't you bring me down today.

REASON
(NO ANGELS)

Words & Music by Thorsten Broetzmann
& Alexander Geringas
Arr.: Hans-Günter Heumann

1. I'm go-ing through good ____

IF TOMORROW NEVER COMES
(RONAN KEATING)

Words & Music by Garth Brooks & Kent Blazy
Arr.: Hans-Günter Heumann

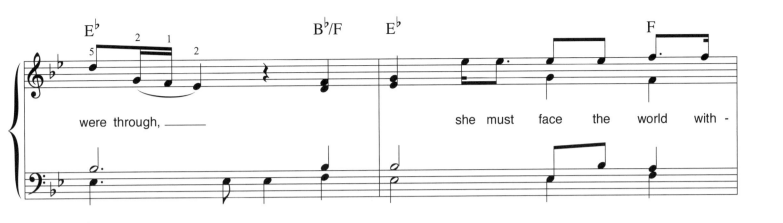

were through, _____ she must face the world with -

out me. Is the love I gave _____ her in the past

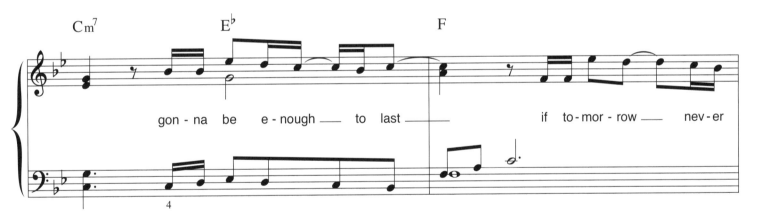

gon - na be e - nough _____ to last _____ if to - mor - row _____ nev - er

comes? _____ 2. 'Cause I've lost loved _____ ones _____ in my

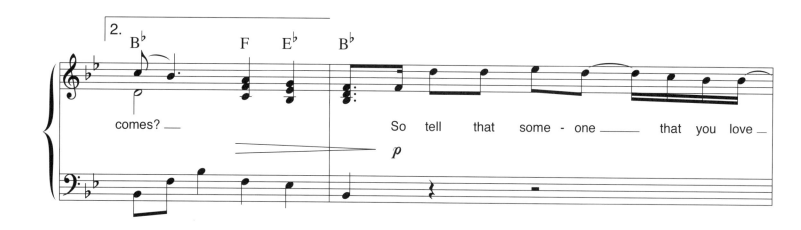

comes? — So tell that some - one ___ that you love ___

p

___ just what you're think-ing of it to-mor-row ___ nev-er

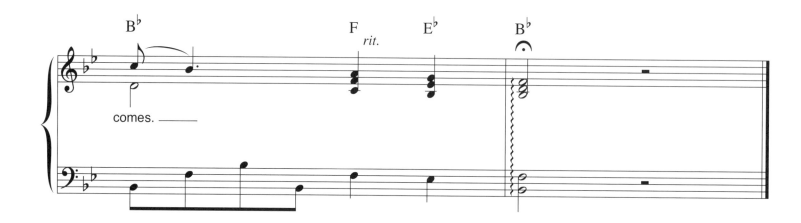

comes. ___

Verse 2:

'Cause I've lost loved ones in my life
who never knew how much I loved them.
Now I live with the regret,
that my true feelings for them never were revealed,
so I made a promise to myself
to say each day how much she means to me,
and avoid that circumstance
where there's no second chance
to tell her how I feel.

If tomorrow never comes ...

WHAT IF
(KATE WINSLET)

Words & Music by Steve McCutcheon & Wayne Hector
Arr.: Hans-Günter Heumann

Verse 2:

Many roads to take,
some to joy, some to heartache.
Anyone can lose their way
and if I said that we could turn it back,
right back to the start.
Would you take the chance and make the change?
Do you think how it would have been sometimes,
do you pray that I'd never left your side.

What if I had never let you go? ...

HERO
(MARIAH CAREY)

Words & Music by Mariah Carey & Walter Afanasieff
Arr.: Hans-Günter Heumann

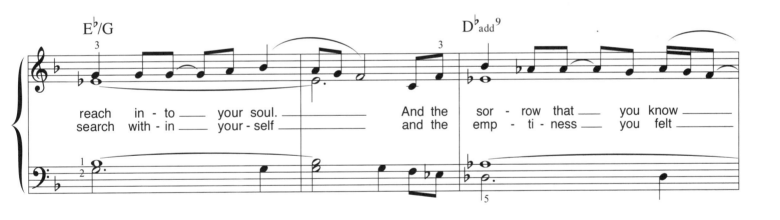

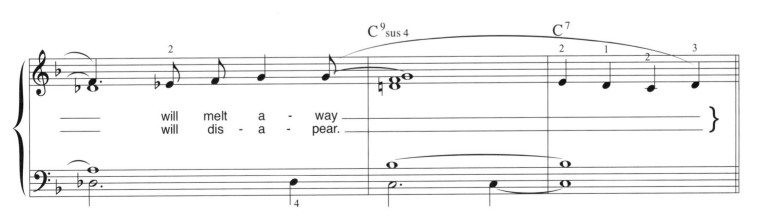

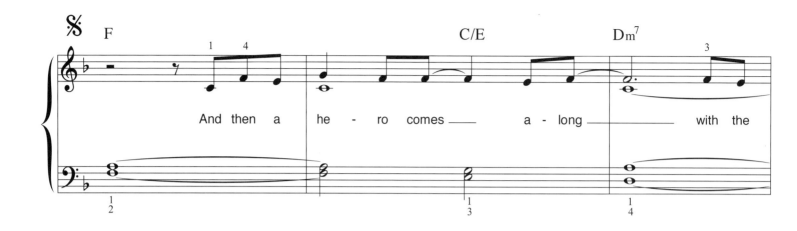

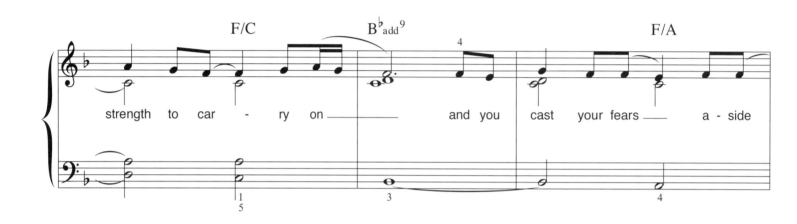

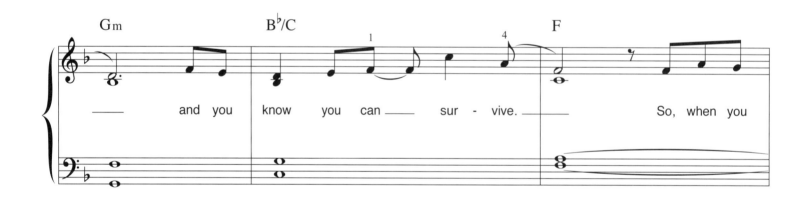

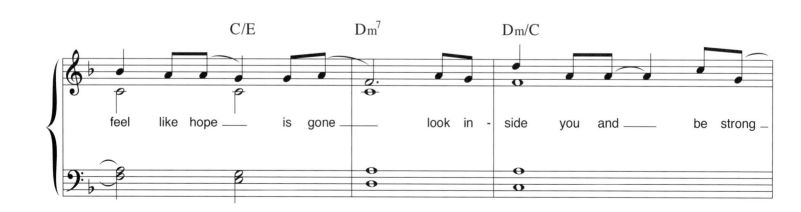

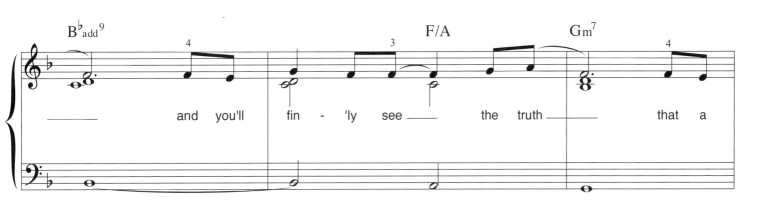

and you'll fin - 'ly see _____ the truth _____ that a

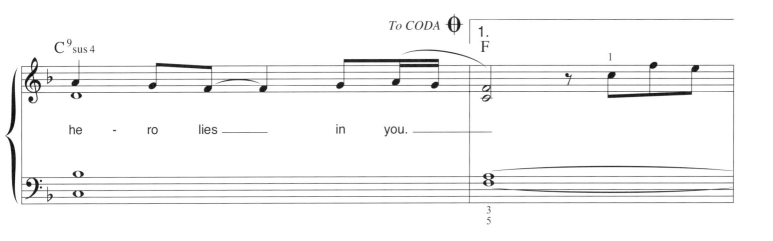

To CODA

he - ro lies _____ in you. _____

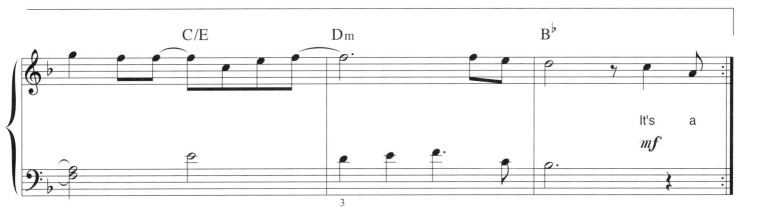

It's a

THREE TIMES A LADY

(LIONEL RICHIE)

Words & Music by Lionel Richie
Arr.: Hans-Günter Heumann

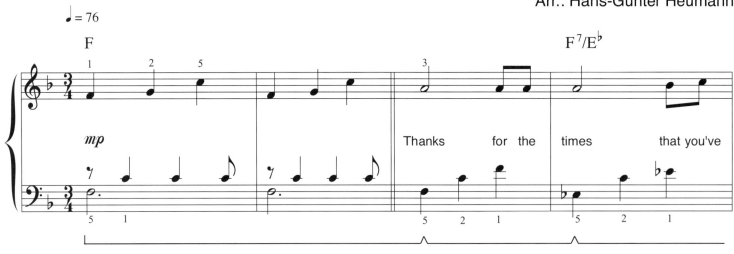

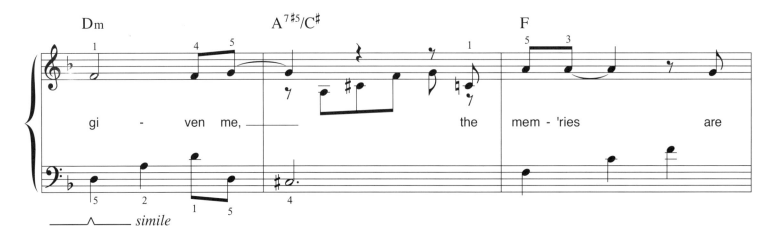

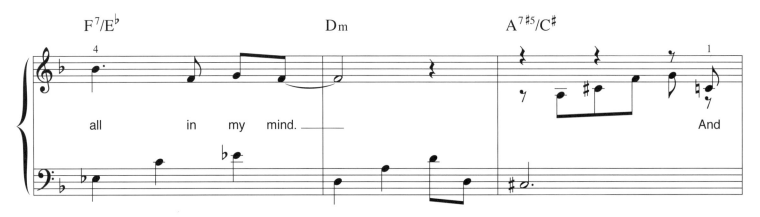

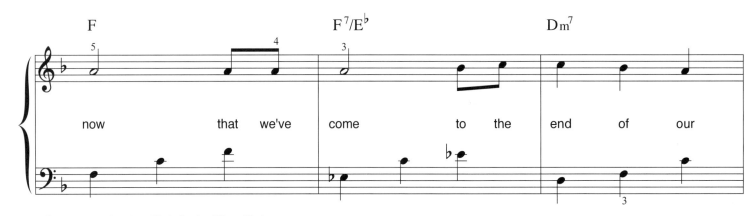

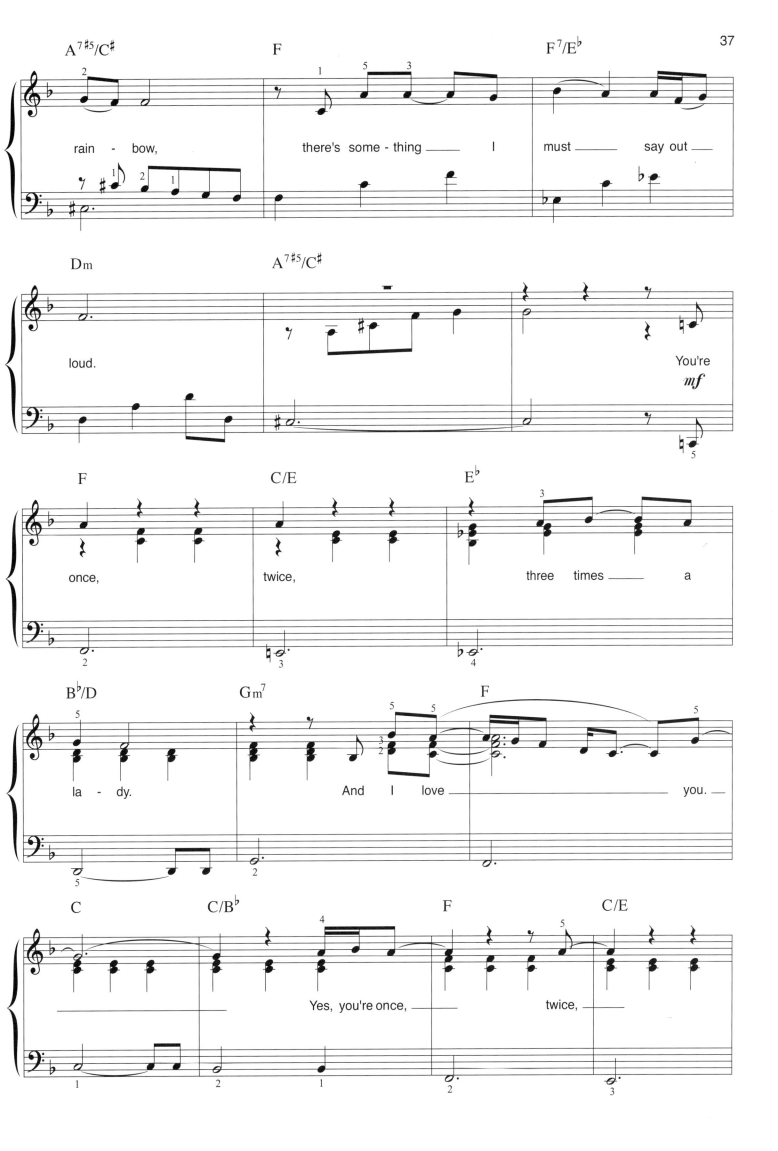

SHE'S THE ONE
(ROBBIE WILLIAMS)

Words & Music by Karl Wallinger
Arr.: Hans-Günter Heumann

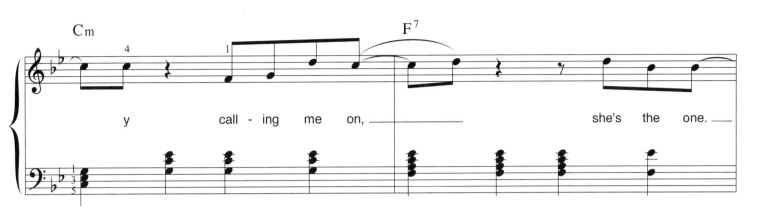

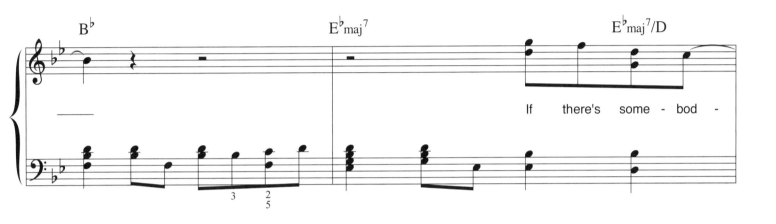

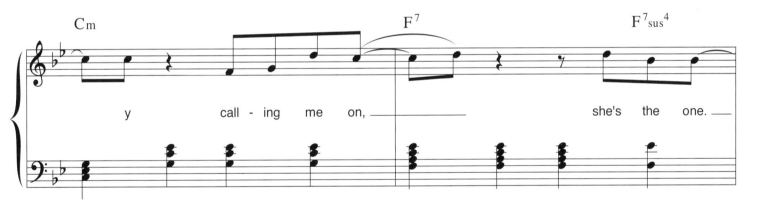

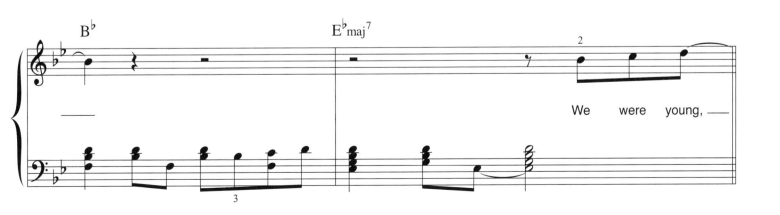

When you get to where you wan-na go, — and you know the things you wan-na know, — you're

smil - ing. —

When you said what you wan-na say — and you know the way you wan-na play, — yeah.

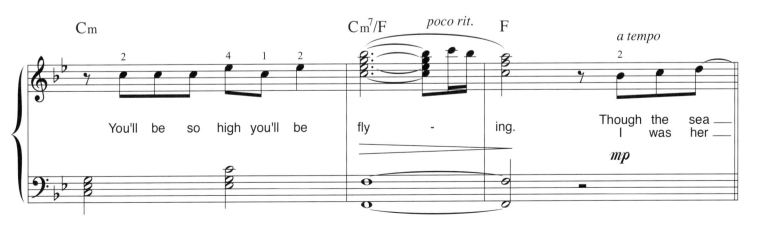

You'll be so high you'll be fly - ing. Though the sea — I was her —

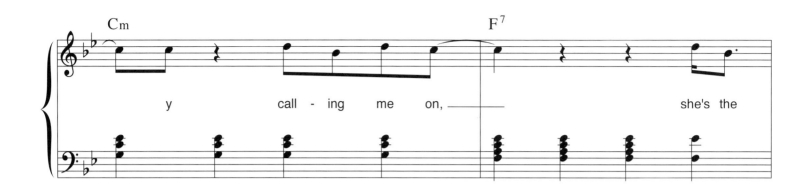

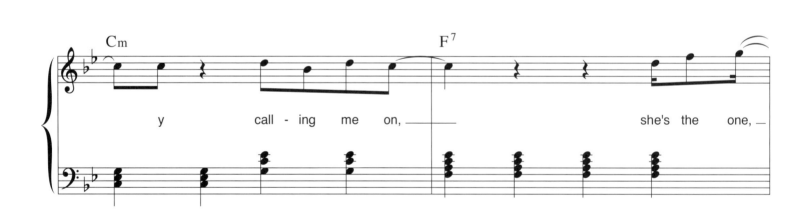

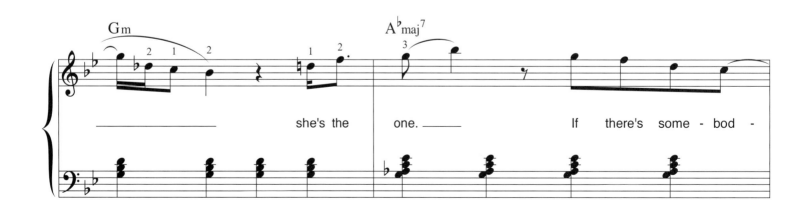

IN MY PLACE
(COLDPLAY)

Words & Music by Guy Berryman, Jon Buckland,
Will Champion & Chris Martin
Arr.: Hans-Günter Heumann

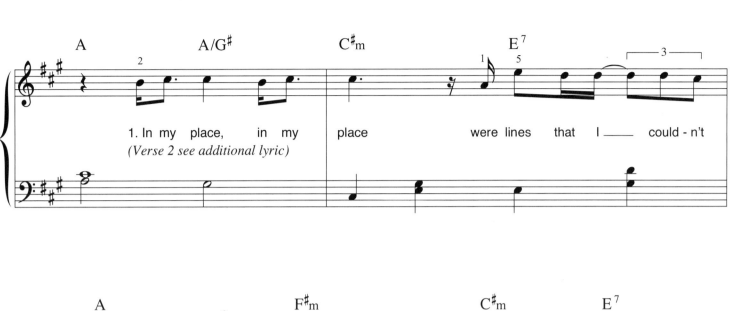

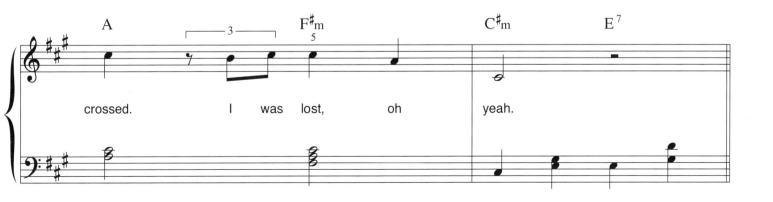

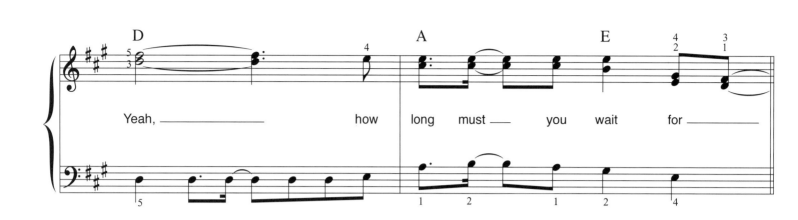

Yeah, _____ how long must _____ you wait for _____

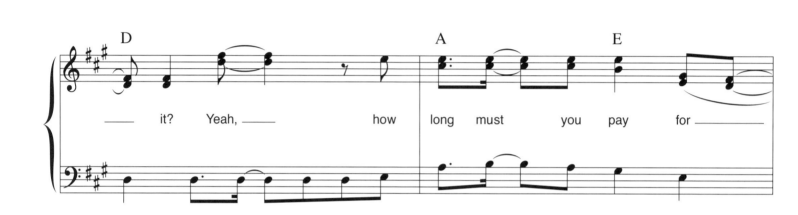

_____ it? Yeah, _____ how long must you pay for _____

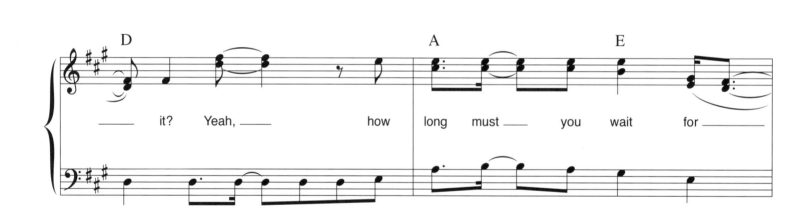

_____ it? Yeah, _____ how long must _____ you wait for _____

_____ it? Ah, for it?

Sing it

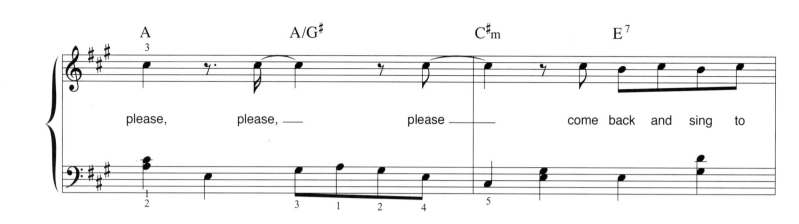

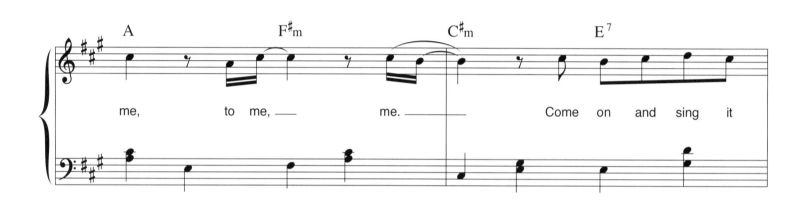

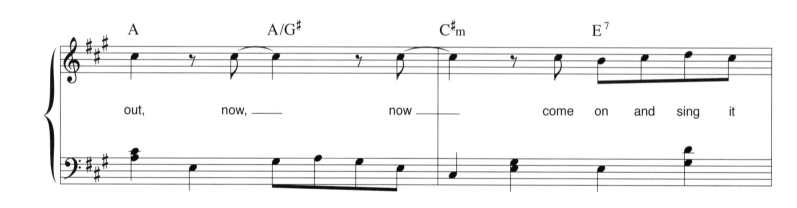

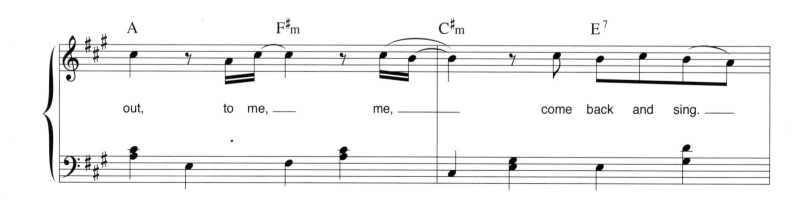

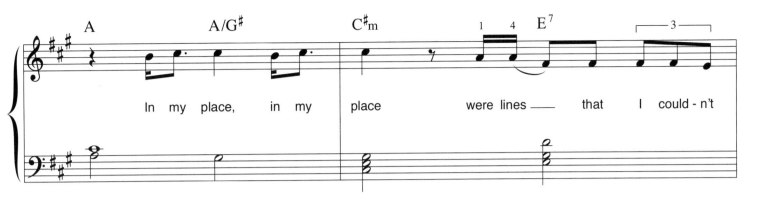

In my place, in my place were lines — that I could-n't

change and I was lost, oh yeah. — Oh — yeah. —

Verse 2:

I was scared, I was scared,
tired and under-prepared
but I'll wait for it.
And if you go, if you go
and leave me down here on my own
then I'll wait for you, yeah.

How long must you wait ...

LOVE IS ALL AROUND
(WET WET WET)

Words & Music by Reg Presley
Arr.: Hans-Günter Heumann

1. I feel it in my fin - gers,
(Verse 2 see additional lyric)

I feel it in my toes. —

love that's all a - round me

and so the feel - ing grows. —

The

love that's all a - round me

and so the feel - ing grows. —

Got to keep it mov - ing.

It's

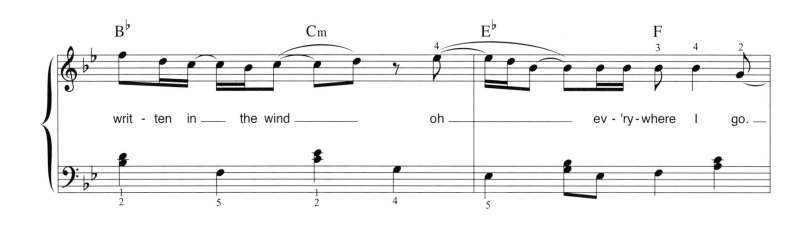

writ - ten in ___ the wind _____ oh _____ ev - 'ry - where I go. ___

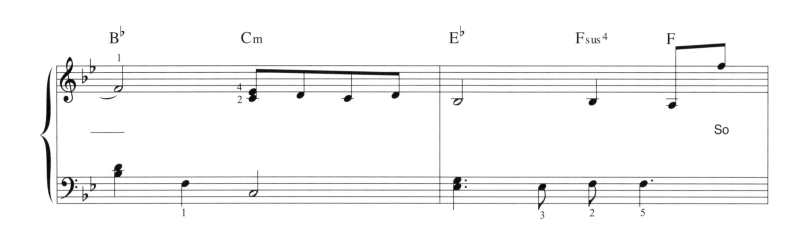

So

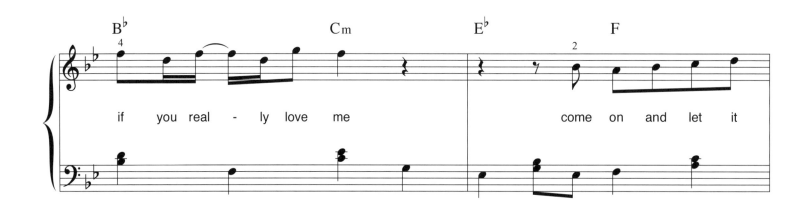

if you real - ly love me _____ come on and let it

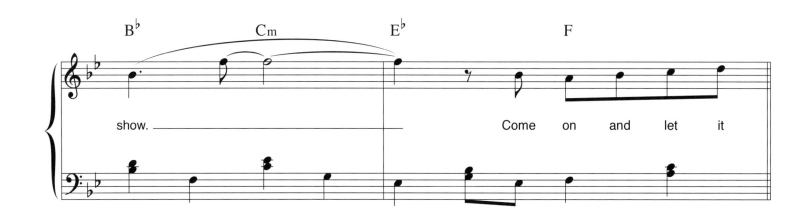

show. _____ Come on and let it

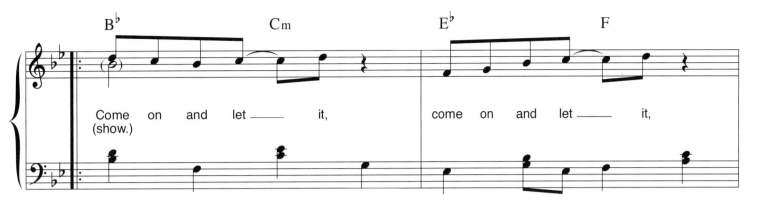

Come on and let —— it,
(show.)
come on and let —— it,

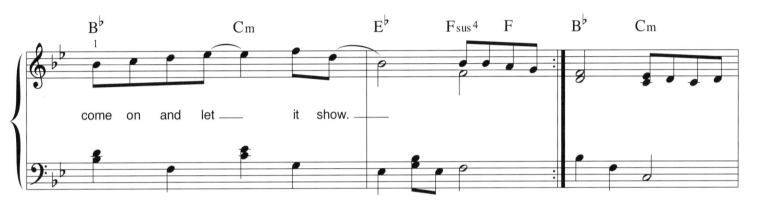

come on and let —— it show. ——

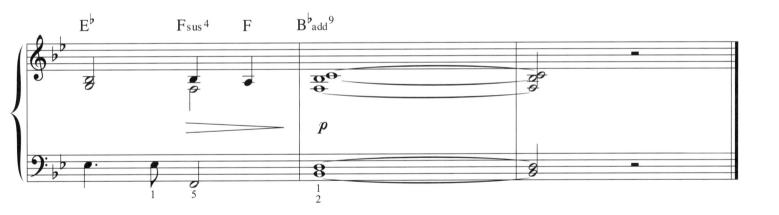

Verse 2:

I see your face before me
as I lay on my bed.
I cannot get to thinking
of all the things you said.
You gave your promise to me
and I gave mine to you.
I need someone beside me
in everything I do.

ANGEL OF BERLIN
(MARTIN KESICI)

Words & Music by Robin Grubert
Arr.: Hans-Günter Heumann

Met her on a stor - my Mon - day, caught up in the mist with - in ___ my - self.

She was on the road to no - where, and I was on the road to no - where

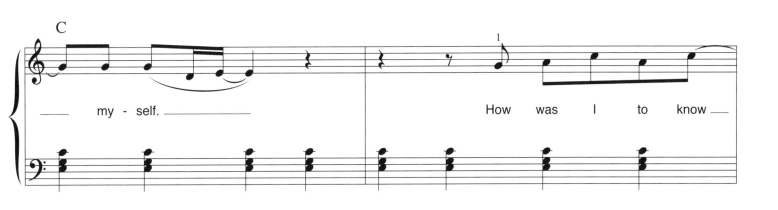

___ my - self. ___ How was I to know ___

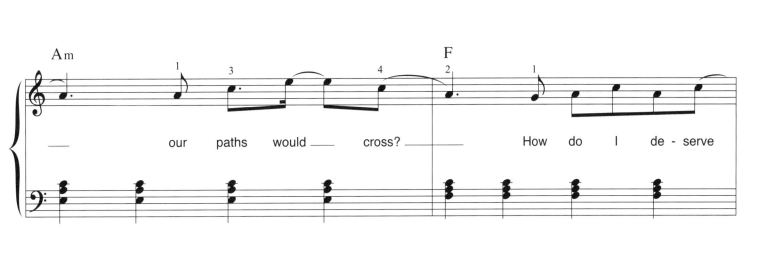

___ our paths would ___ cross? ___ How do I de - serve

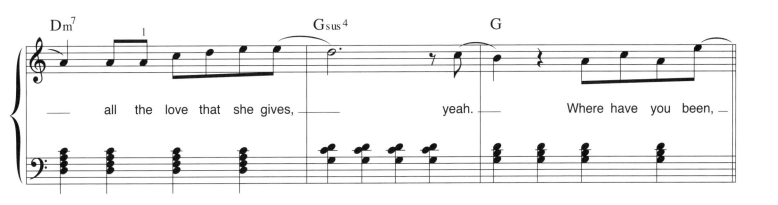

___ all the love that she gives, ___ yeah. ___ Where have you been, ___

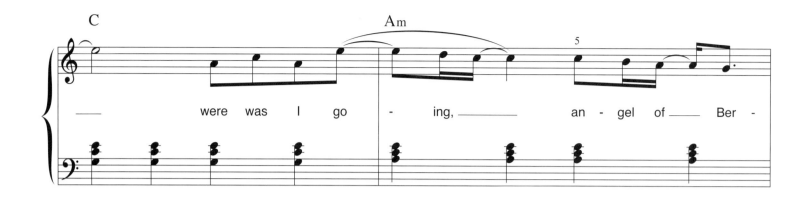

were was I go - ing, _____ an - gel of _____ Ber -

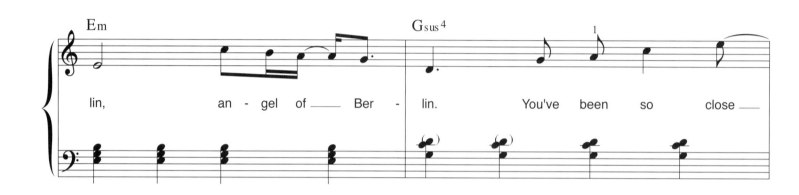

lin, an - gel of _____ Ber - lin. You've been so close _____

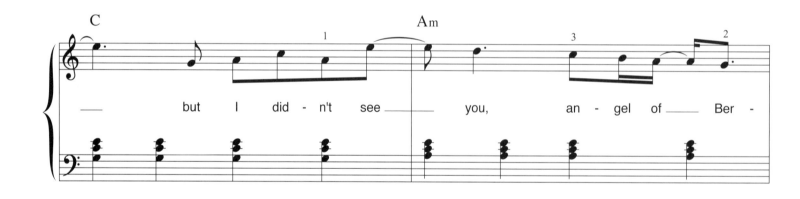

_____ but I did - n't see _____ you, an - gel of _____ Ber -

lin, an - gel of _____ Ber - lin.

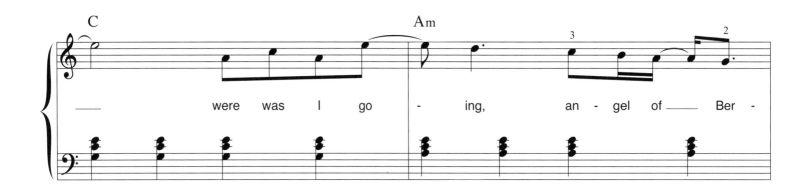

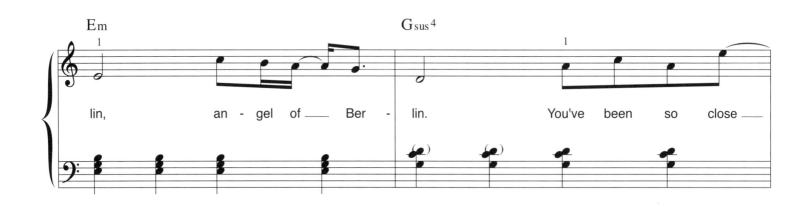

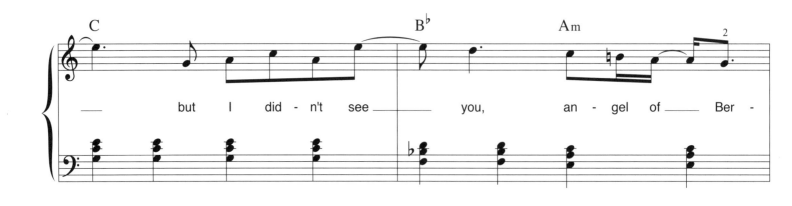

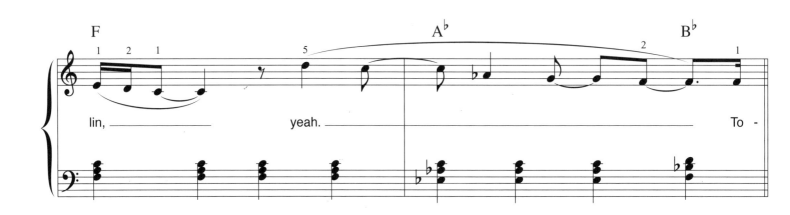

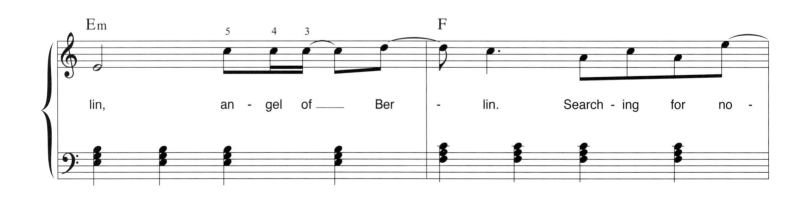

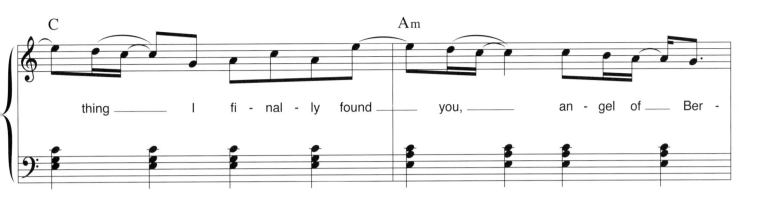

thing ____ I fi - nal - ly found ____ you, ____ an - gel of ___ Ber -

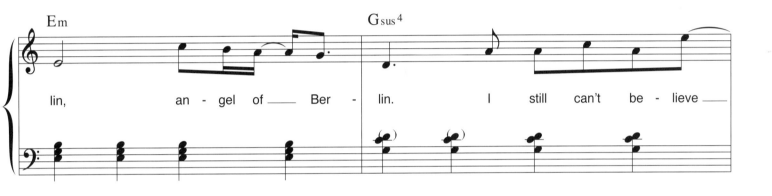

lin, an - gel of ___ Ber - lin. I still can't be - lieve ____

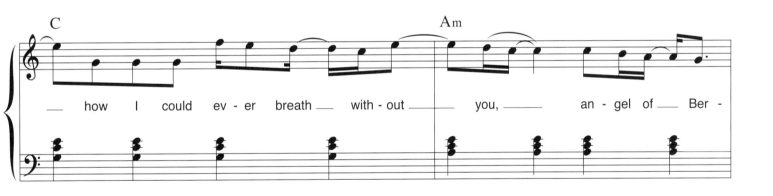

___ how I could ev - er breath ___ with - out ____ you, ____ an - gel of ___ Ber -

lin. _____

ONE FLIGHT DOWN
(NORAH JONES)

Words & Music by Jesse Harris
Arr.: Hans-Günter Heumann

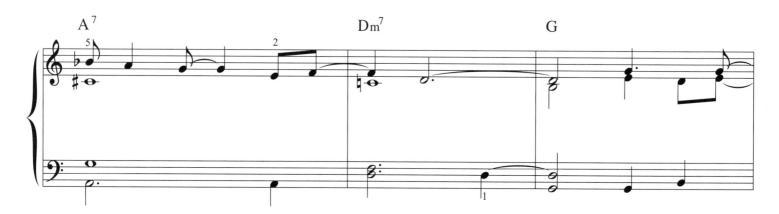

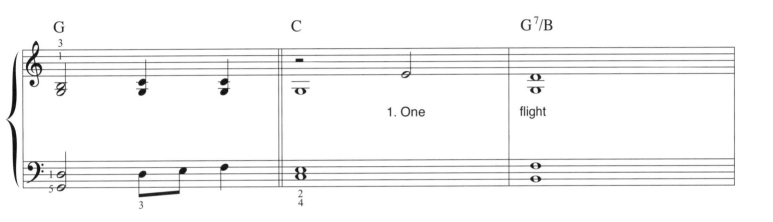

1. One flight

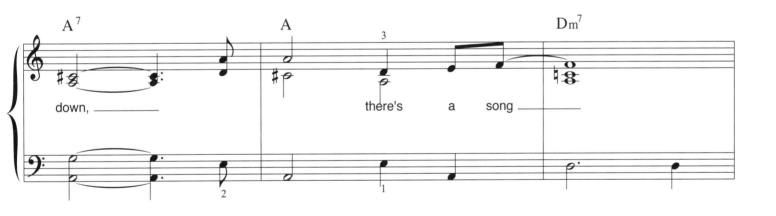

down, there's a song

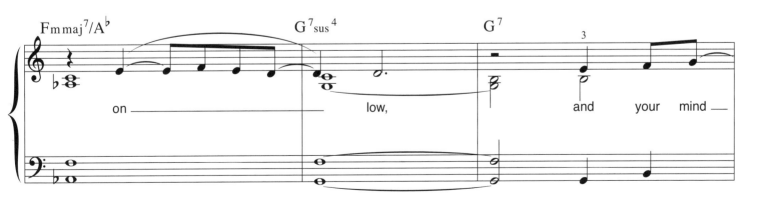

on low, and your mind

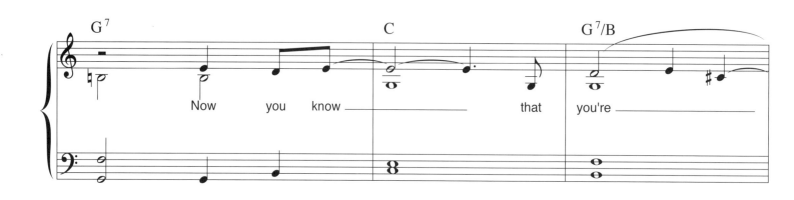

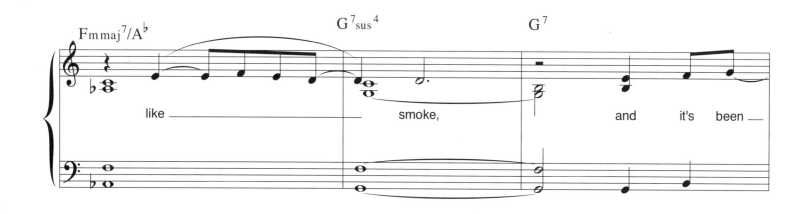

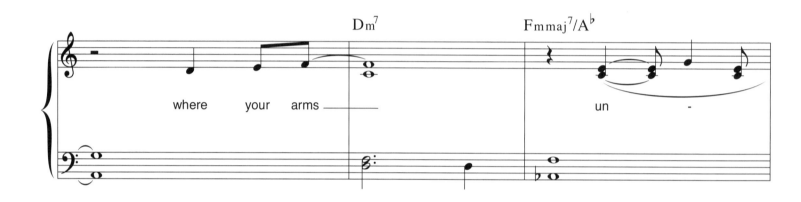

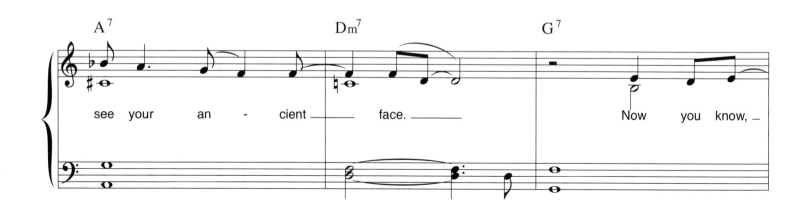

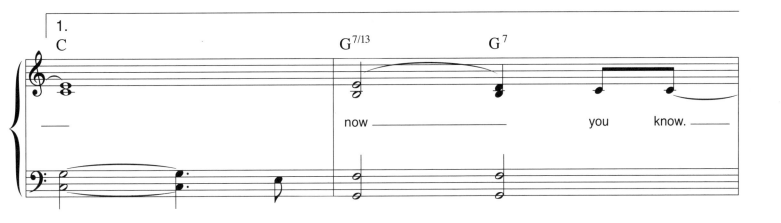

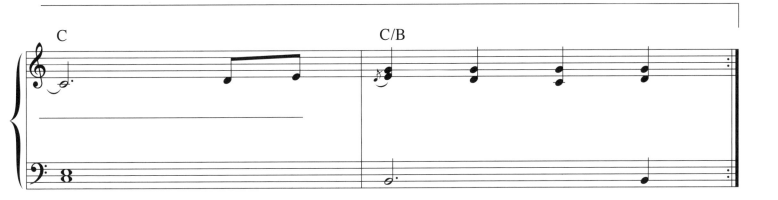

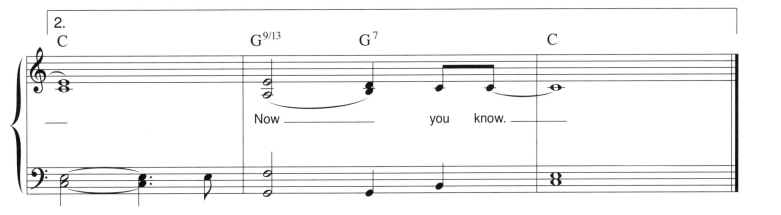

Verse 3:

The cadence rolls in broken,
plays it over and then goes.
One flight down,
there's a song on low,
and it's been there playing all along,
now you know,
now you know .

STOP CRYING YOUR HEART OUT
(OASIS)

Words & Music by Noel Gallagher
Arr.: Hans-Günter Heumann

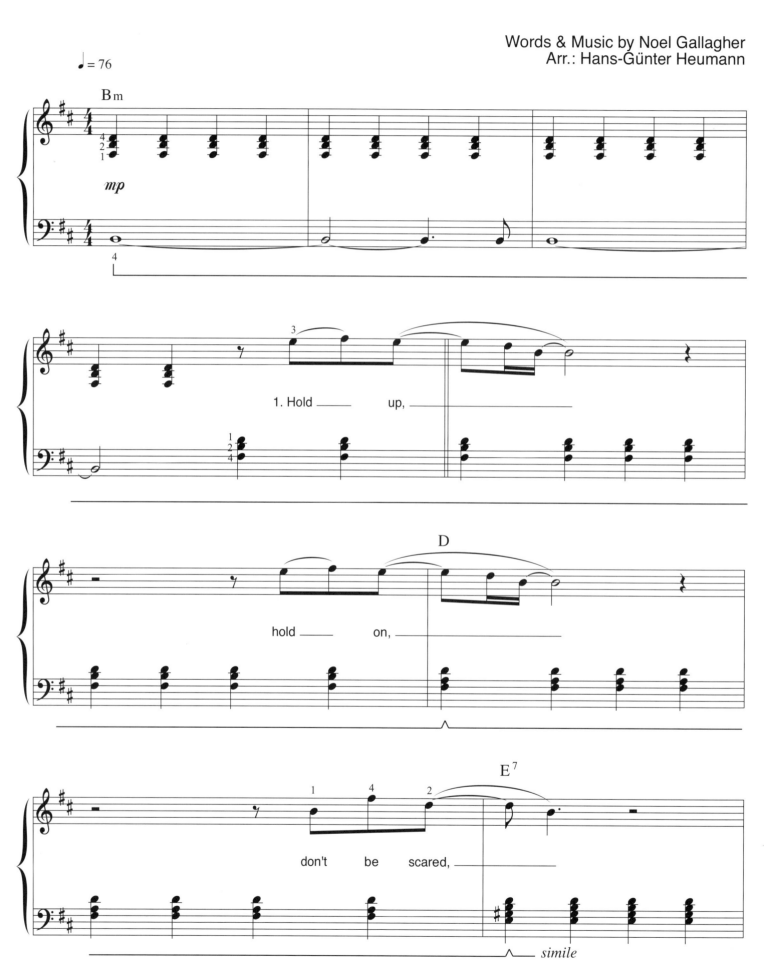

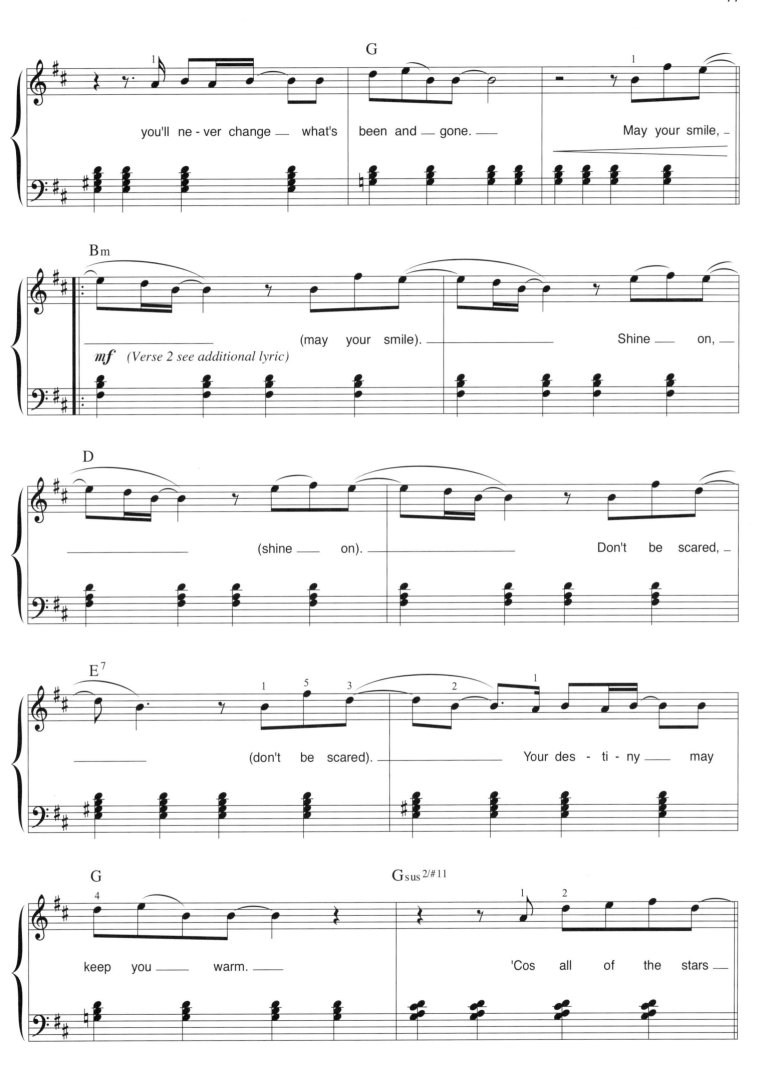

Verse 2:

Get up, come on,
why're you scared?
(I'm not scared.)
You'll never change what's been and gone.

'Cos all of the stars ...

IF I COULD TURN BACK
THE HANDS OF TIME

(R. KELLY)

Words & Music by Robert Kelly
Arr.: Hans-Günter Heumann

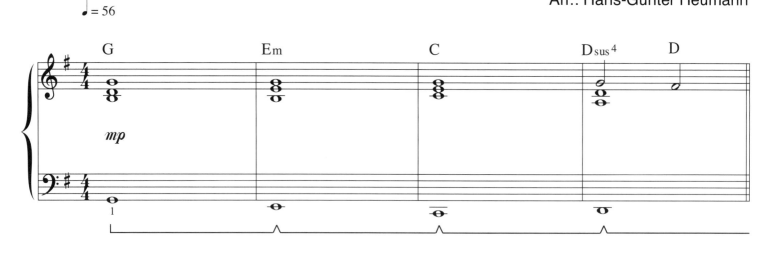

How did I ev-er let you slip a-way, nev-er know-ing I'd be sing-ing this

song some-day? And now I'm sink-ing, sink-ing to rise no more,

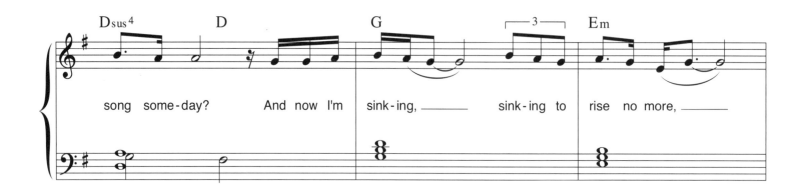

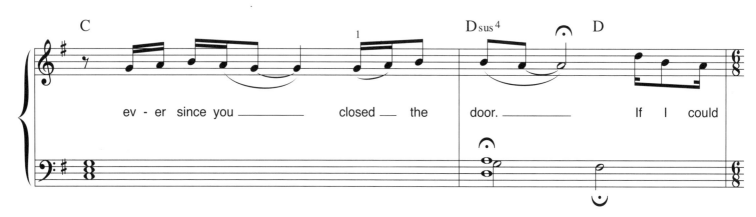

ev-er since you closed the door. If I could

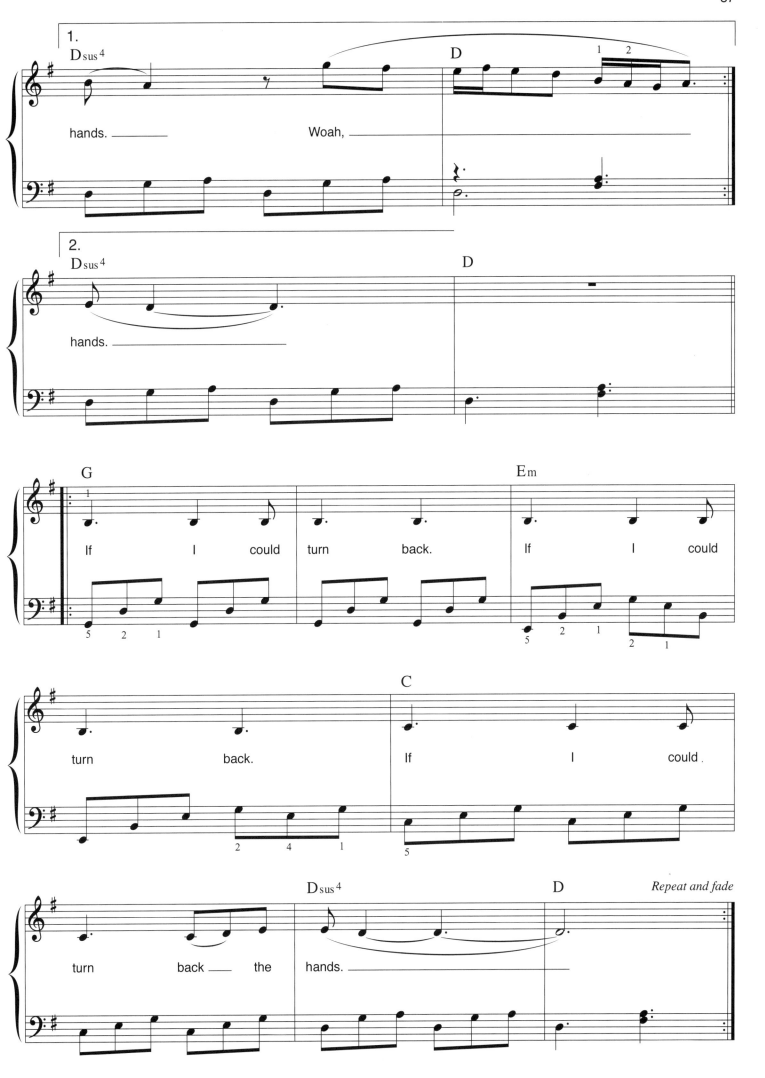

HARD TO SAY I'M SORRY

(CHICAGO)

Words & Music by Peter Cetera &
David Walter Foster
Arr.: Hans-Günter Heumann

Ev-'ry-bo-dy   needs a lit-tle time a-way,   I heard her say _

93

I WON'T HOLD YOU BACK
(TOTO)

Words & Music by Steve Lukather
Arr.: Hans-Günter Heumann

If I had _____ an - oth - er chance _____ to - night,
Now you're gone; _____ I'm real - ly not _____ the same.

I'd try _____ to tell _____ you that _____ the things
I guess _____ I have _____ my - self _____ to blame.

TAKE MY BREATH AWAY
(BERLIN)

Words by Tom Whitlock
Music by Giorgio Moroder
Arr.: Hans-Günter Heumann

1. Watch-ing ev-'ry mo-tion in ___ my fool-ish lov-er's game, ___

(Verses 2 & 3 see additional lyric)

on this end-less oc-ean, fin-

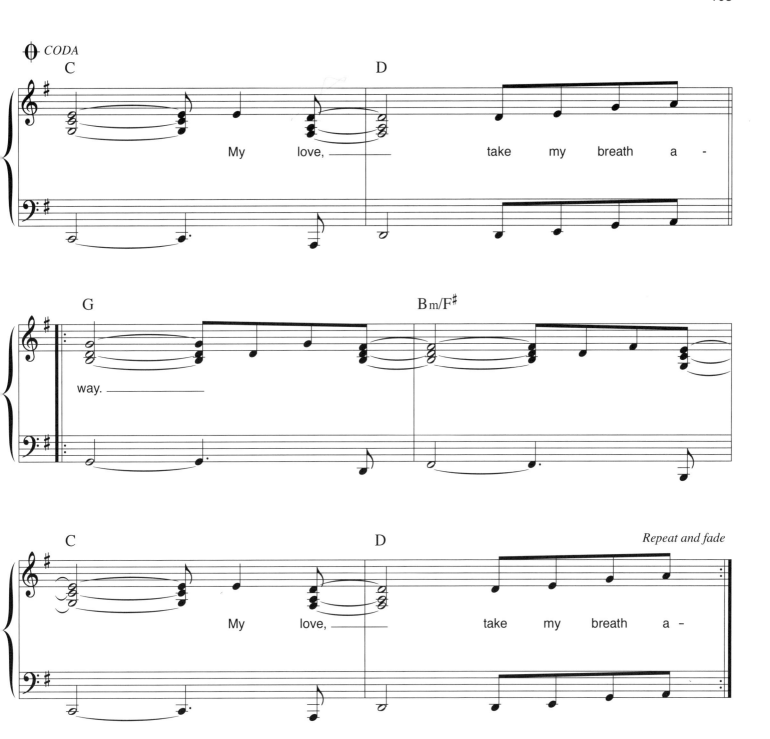

Verse 2:

Watching, I keep waiting, still anticipating love,
never hesitating to become the fated ones.
Turning and returning to some secret place to hide,
watching in slow motion as you turn to me and say:

"Take my breath away ..."

Verse 3:

Watching every motion in this foolish lover's game,
haunted by the notion somewhere there's a love in flames.
Turning and returning to some secret place inside,
watching in slow motion as you turn to me and say:

"Take my breath away ..."

A GROOVY KIND OF LOVE
(PHIL COLLINS)

Words & Music by Toni Wine & Carole Bayer-Sager
Arr.: Hans-Günter Heumann

1. When I'm fee - lin' blue, all I have to
(Verse 2 see additional lyric)
do Is take a look at you, then I'm not so blue. When you're close to

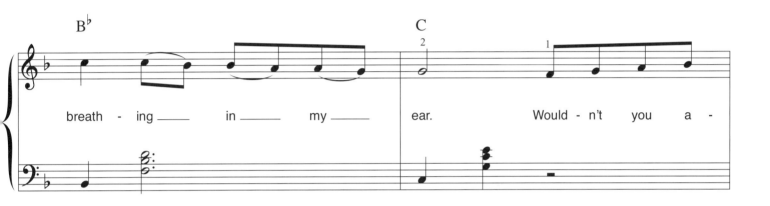

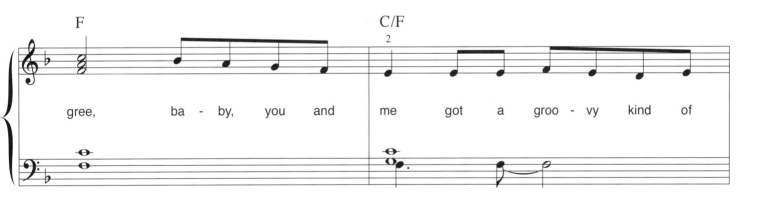

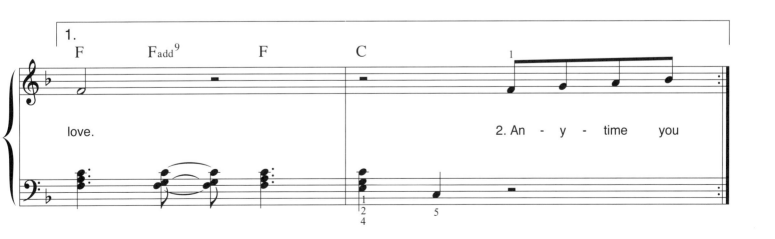

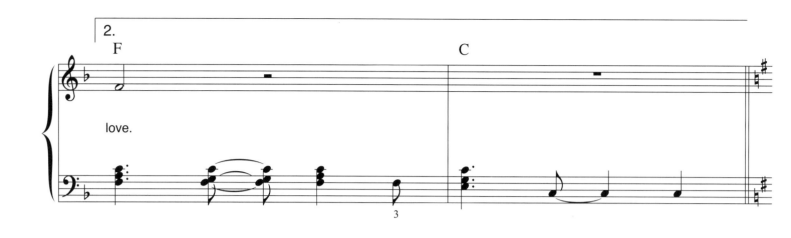

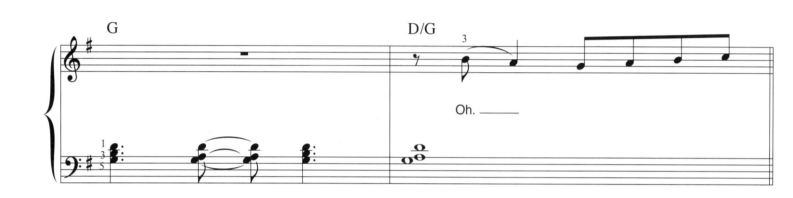

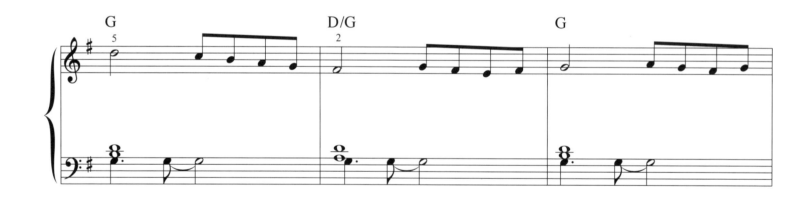

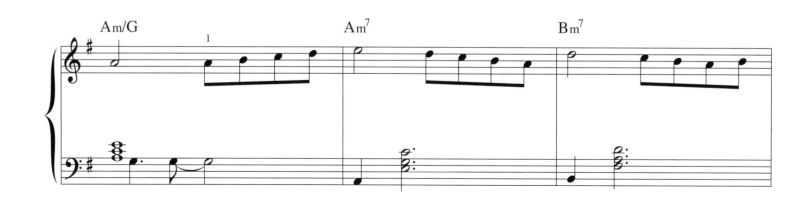

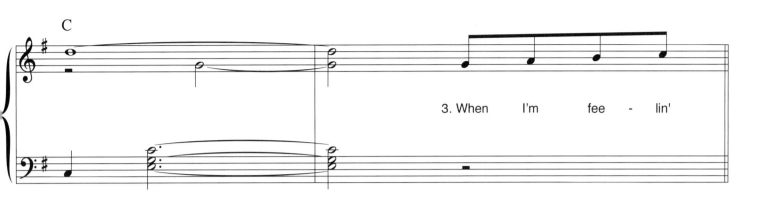

C

3. When I'm fee - lin'

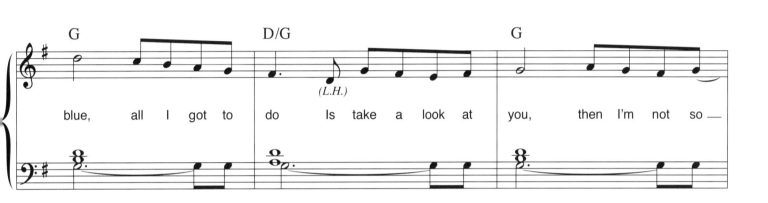

G   D/G   G

blue, all I got to do Is take a look at you, then I'm not so —

(L.H.)

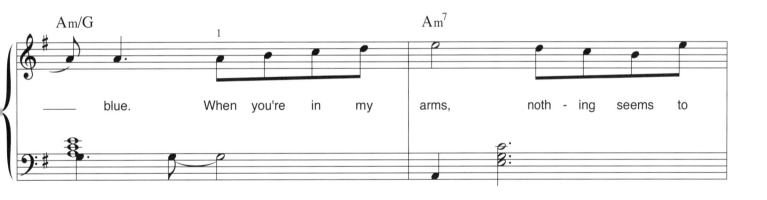

Am/G   Am7

— blue. When you're in my arms, noth - ing seems to

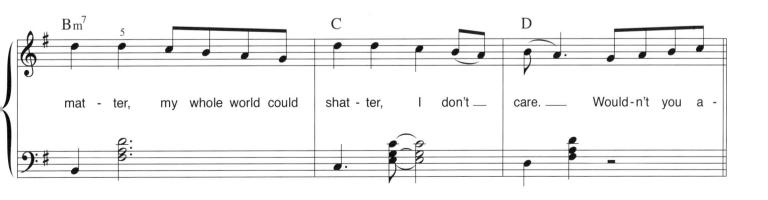

Bm7   C   D

mat - ter, my whole world could shat - ter, I don't — care. — Would-n't you a -

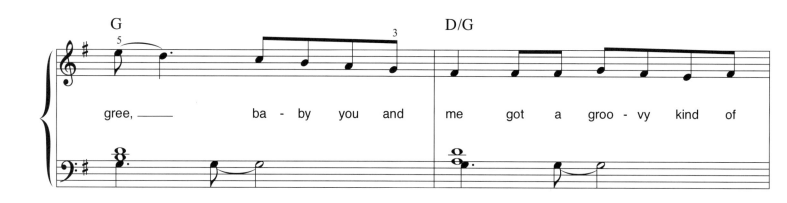

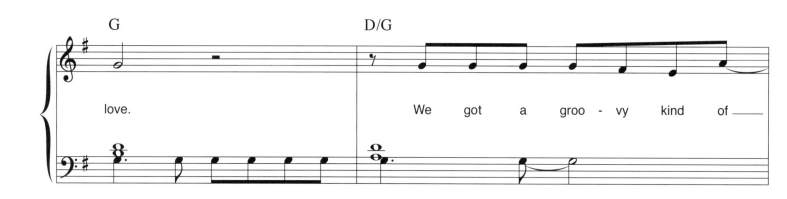

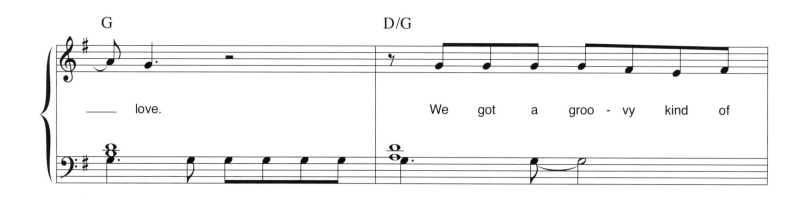

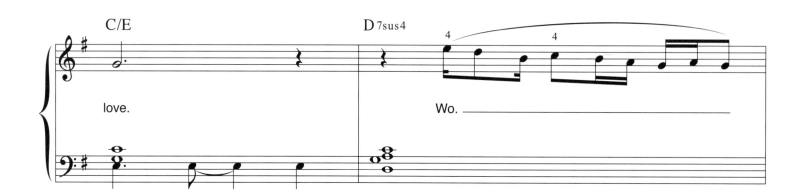

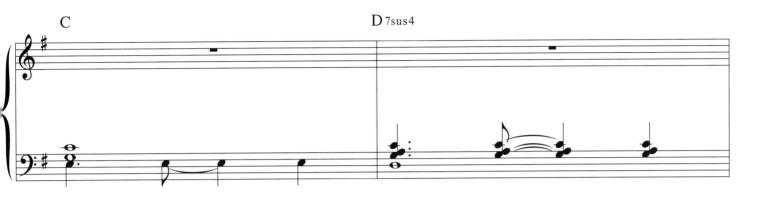

We got a groo - vy kind of love.

Verse 2:

Anything you want to,
you can turn me on
to anything you want to,
anytime at all.
When I kiss your lips,
ooh, I start to shiver,
can't control the quivering inside.
Wouldn't you agree,
baby, you and me
got a groovy kind of love.

SORRY SEEMS TO BE THE HARDEST WORD

(ELTON JOHN)

Words & Music by Elton John & Bernie Taupin
Arr.: Hans-Günter Heumann

What have I got to do to make you love me?

What have I got to do to make you care?

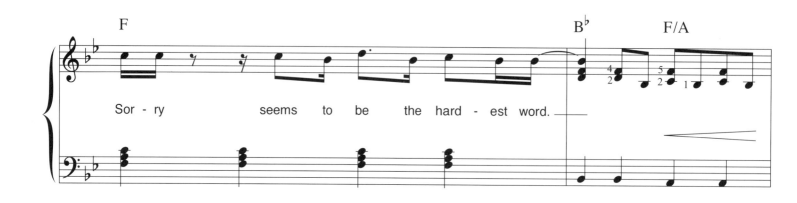

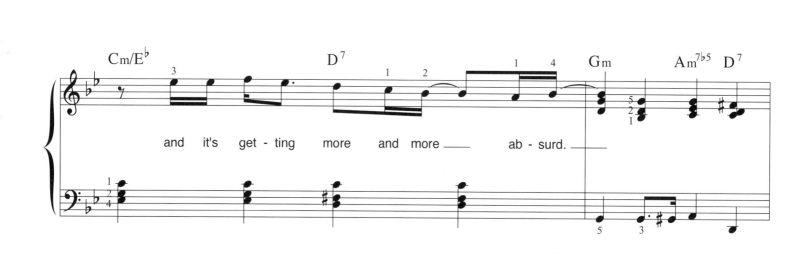

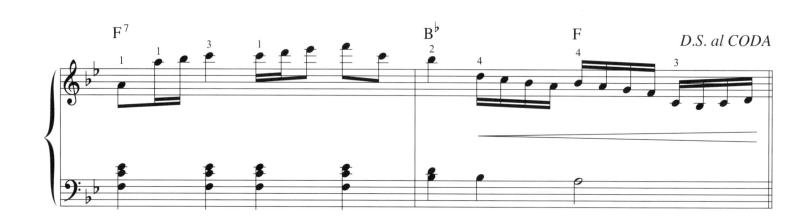

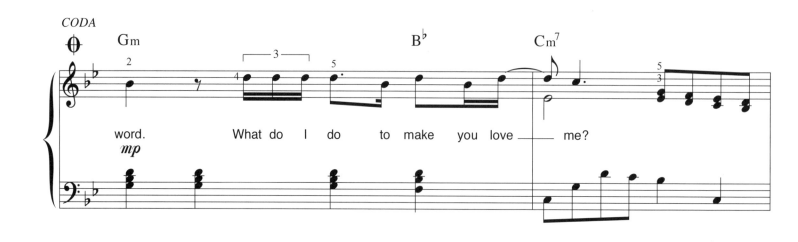

E♭/G D/F♯ B♭/F C7/E
It's sad, it's so sad why can't we talk it o - ver?
E♭ Cm7 D7
To CODA
Al - ways seems to me that sor - ry seems to be the hard - est
Gm Cm
word.
mp
F7 E♭ F7 B♭ Am7♭5 D7

word. What do I do to make you love _____ me?

What have I got to do _____ to be heard?

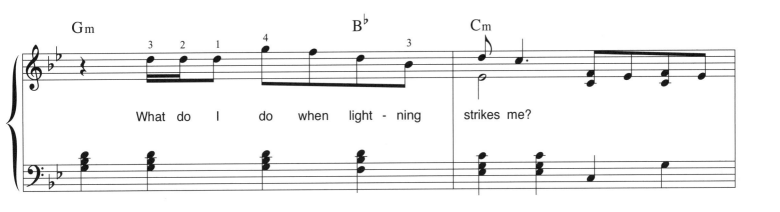

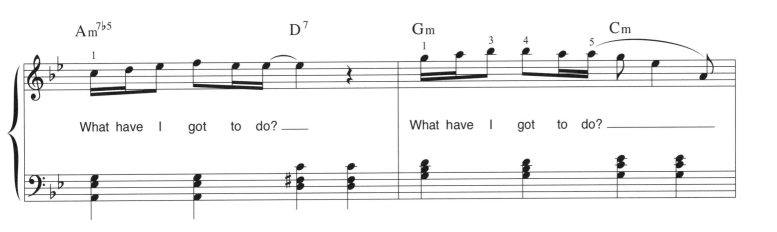

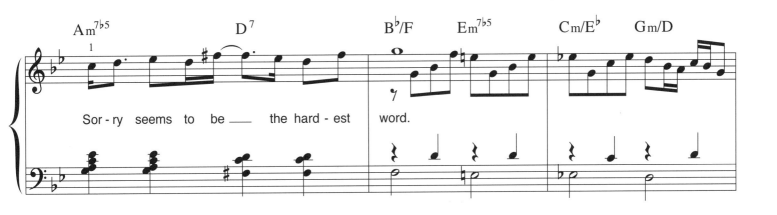

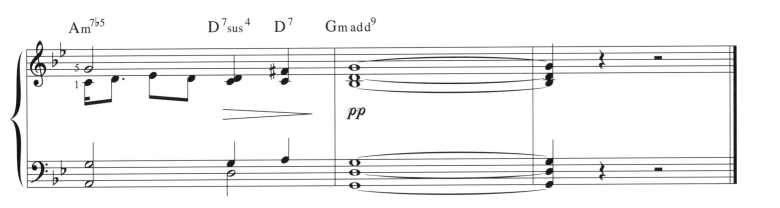

YOU ARE SO BEAUTIFUL
(JOE COCKER)

Words & Music by Billy Preston & Bruce Fisher
Arr.: Hans-Günter Heumann

Lyrics: You are so beau-ti-ful ___ to me.

You are ___ so beau - ti - ful ___

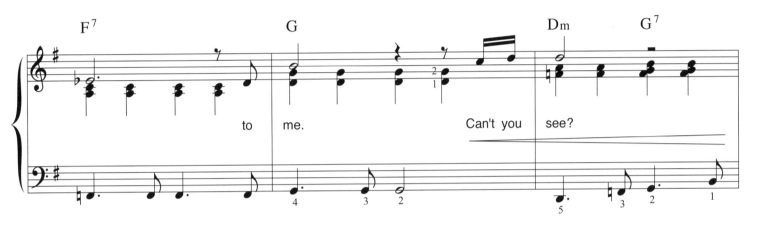

to me. Can't you see?

You're ___ ev - 'ry - thing I hope ___ for, you're

ev - 'ry - thing I need. ___

Made in the EU 3/08 (165251)